D0955807

The
Zombie
Handbook

First edition for North America published in 2011 by
Barron's Educational Series, Inc.

All inquiries should be addressed to:
Barron's Educational Series, Inc.
250 Wireless Boulevard
Hauppauge, NY 11788
www.barronseduc.com

ISBN 13: 978-0-7641-6409-5
ISBN 10: 0-7641-6409-0
Library of Congress Control Number:
2010931488

M ZOM

Conceived, designed, and produced by
Marshall Editions
The Old Brewery
6 Blundell Street
London N7 9BH
www.marshalleditions.com

Commissioning Editors: Laura Price, Miranda Smith
Project Editor: Gill Denton
Design: Duncan Brown – The Book Makers
Picture Manager: Veneta Bullen
Production: Nikki Ingram

Date of manufacture: March 2011
Manufactured by: 1010 Printing International Ltd.
Color separation by: Modern Age Repro House Ltd.,
Hong Kong

Printed in China

10 9 8 7 6 5 4 3 2 1

The ZOMBIE HANDBOOK

Dr. Robert Curran

BARRON'S

Contents

What Is a Zombie?

This is a difficult question to answer, because the definitions of "zombie" are many and varied. It is often taken to be a part of Voodoo belief, usually connected with the Caribbean, and to refer to a walking dead body raised from the grave by sorcery.

In the oldest Voodoo beliefs the word "Zombi" does not refer to the dead at all but means a great serpent that is the symbol of Damballah Wedo, chief of all the Voodoo gods. In more modern times the word refers to a shambling, mindless corpse, often controlled by magic, and subject to the will of whoever raised it from the dead. According to legend, the awful resurrection may be done through spells and incantations or by murdering someone using a special deadly potion. This brings them back to a semblance of life after they are dead.

LEFT *Two zombies emerge from the shadows looking for their next meal.*

ABOVE *Traditional zombie field workers. Cobwebs don't take very long to take hold of the living dead.*

The idea of the zombie as the walking dead does not, however, appear only in Caribbean folklore. The term may also refer to the mummy, which forms a part of Egyptian tradition and is a bandage-swathed, living-dead figure that can be raised by powerful magic; or to the ghoul of Arabian nightmare, a dead being that lies underground during the day and emerges at night to torment the living; and even to the marbh bheo of Ireland, the nightwalking corpses who arise from their lonely graves to walk the Irish roads under a full moon.

But it is in places like Haiti and parts of the southern states of America where the zombie tradition – that of the shambling, decaying human figure – has gained the greatest hold, particularly in the regions where slavery was once practiced. The lonely roads through the swamps in remote areas are often the haunt of strange, awkward shadows, and who knows what these might be? You have been warned!

How Do They Look?

Now, we know that zombies are the dead who have risen from their graves. Therefore, to look at in their decayed and decaying state, they are often indistinguishable from one another. Although their appearance may sometimes vary slightly, mostly they all have the same characteristics.

If they have not been too long in the ground, they may be recognizable as the person who has been buried. However, their skins are often dark from grave earth, and their hair and fingernails might be long, giving them a wild, menacing appearance. But it is often their eyes that are the most frightening – they are large, bright points of light, but they always have a vacant, dead stare because there is no intelligence behind them.

LEFT *The undead rise from their coffins for a night of feeding, and spot a passerby. Unlucky man!*

All zombies move with a jerky, almost robot-like gait, manipulated from afar by some controlling priest or priestess. Some sources say that zombies have large, animal-like teeth for eating human flesh. But this is probably a modern theory taken from movies and books; there is no suggestion in folklore that zombies are flesh-eating.

Some zombies can be recognized by their clothing. In various beliefs – for example in Rada Voodoo – zombies are possessed by the *loa*, or spirit of a god, and this can give them certain characteristics of manner and clothing. For example, a corpse occupied by the *loa* of Baron Cemetière (Lord of the Graveyards and Master of the Unquiet Dead) appears as a skeleton dressed in a shabby tuxedo and top hat, often smoking a cigarette in a long holder. Another *loa*, Shago (who can control storms, and especially lightning), appears as a soldier in a stained and torn uniform.

Other spirits adopt slightly different forms when they decide to occupy dead bodies.

In whatever circumstances, if you are approached by a drooling, earth-smeared zombie, there is no chance you won't recognize it immediately. You must run!

BELOW *Baron Cemetière (sometimes known as Baron Samedi) had several names and was believed to have been adopted by practitioners of Voodoo from ancient Celtic pagan beliefs.*

WHERE ARE THEY FROM?

No matter where you go in the world, there's a chance that you will run into the walking dead. Nearly every country has lore about the returning dead — maybe not exactly in the conventional zombie form, but really not all that different.

The zombie that we are most familiar with comes, of course, from the Caribbean and is to be found in places such as Haiti, where slaves were taken from Africa and South America to work in the plantations. The slaves brought with them, from West Africa, tales of the walking dead that terrified the white planters. In places such as Dahomey (now Benin) and the Congo Basin there are many frightening stories of the walking dead, who can be called back to "life" from their graves to do the bidding of witch doctors and shamans.

In parts of North America, in southern states such as Louisiana and South Carolina where slaves have settled, there too has settled the zombie. Tucked away in the remote swamplands and bayous, perhaps in some isolated cemetery or crumbling antebellum (pre-Civil War) mansion, one might find the *zuvembe* – a creature that is not quite dead but which has all the appearance of a zombie.

But it is not only in the U.S.A. where stories about the walking dead can be found. In countries such as Mexico, the dead sometimes leave their tombs to consort with the living. In many parts of Latin America the people even have a special festival for this – The Day of the Dead – when there is great feasting, and during which the dead may put in an appearance.

On a much more sinister note, in parts of Ireland, the marbh bheo are thought to wander the gloomy roads as the sun is going down, often for mysterious purposes. And in Palermo, Sicily, in a Capuchin crypt, thousands of mummified dead are reputed to be zombies. So no matter where you are, look over your shoulder from time to time. A zombie might be behind you!

BELOW *In a Sicilian catacomb, beautifully dressed mummies of monks and others may be waiting to rise from the dead.*

HOW TO SPOT A ZOMBIE

Because a zombie is really a corpse that has risen from the grave, you might think that it would be fairly easy to spot, but this might not always be the case.

Bear in mind, the zombie has usually been called up by a magician or priest who may also be able to disguise it so that it can mingle with living people. This was apparently quite common in former times on the slave plantations, when the living and zombie workers were said to work together. The use of the living dead was a secret from the authorities. There were, however, telltale signs. The first clue was that, according to some, the zombie never speaks, so it cannot answer a direct question. If it does speak (and some traditions said that it can utter a few words), then it does so in a flat, droning voice with no inflection. It sounds very much like a robot, not a human.

Secondly, most zombies have the same vacant and unintelligent stare. They look straight ahead as if seeing nothing. The exception is when zombies are possessed by a *loa* or spirit that can sometimes give them the appearance of life, but this type of zombie is very rare.

Thirdly, a zombie will usually wear ill-fitting clothes, sometimes several sizes too small or too big. The reason for this is that they have been buried in smart burial clothes and when they emerge from the tomb they have to be clothed in someone else's everyday attire. However, this is not always the case, so you can't be too careful.

LEFT Zombies look dirty and unkempt, because they have risen from the earth. Many believe that after a time God will take the soul back, so the zombie state is only temporary.

Lastly, there is the smell. Because zombies have been buried for a time and their bodies have started to decay, they give off a rather unpleasant odor. Some people say that dead bodies, if they are left for quite a while before burial, may smell the same. That is why in some religions, particularly in hot countries, people are buried soon after death. But again, do beware, the person suspected of being a zombie might simply not have washed him- or herself for a very long time.

Remember, zombies can be anywhere – not just in some faraway land. Take a look at the person sitting next to you – you really never know!

HOW TO AVOID A ZOMBIE

If you want to stay out of the way of a lumbering dead person, how do you go about it? The first thing you need to realize is — it's not that easy!

Because a zombie has most probably been raised by sorcery (and quite complicated sorcery at that), it will take a spell or ritual to either confuse it or to drive it away. That said, there are charms that are known as *gris-gris* that might give some sort of protection. The word, which possibly comes from the language of the Bambara people of Mali in Africa, refers to a bag filled with certain powders and charms that you wear around your neck. The bag can contain herbs, the foot of a black cockerel (particularly effective), and sometimes the dust of a dead body. It is also known as a *ju-ju* bag or *mojo*, but be warned – it is really only

ABOVE *A black cockerel. Stones, bones, and nails can also be used for protection.*

effective against zombies from the Caribbean or New Orleans, and it can only be obtained from a real sorcerer at a high price.

A less expensive way to protect yourself is to surround yourself with a ring of salt. Since very early times, salt has been seen as a great protector by many cultures throughout the world, and it is thought that no zombie can cross the salt without doing harm to itself. Nevertheless, the salt ring is not always reliable, and in any case the zombie (which is tireless and never rests) can wait patiently until you have to come out from the salt ring – and then seize you.

Another way that you can avoid the clutches of the undead may be to make sure that there is fresh, running water between you and the zombie. It is widely believed that the dead cannot cross fresh, flowing water, so it may act as a protective barrier. But stagnant or "dead" water won't work because the zombie will easily be able to cross that. All these defenses may or may not help you. The best – and possibly only – way to avoid the zombie is to try and stay well away from it!

BELOW *Zombies don't like fresh, running water. Even running tap water can be enough to repel them.*

ZOMBIE ATTACK

According to the folklore of many cultures, the dead are not terribly fond of the living. Indeed, it might be true to say that they hate them and seek to do them harm if they can.

This innate hatred is often used by the magicians who raise zombies and turn them against the living for their own ends. Dark magic can often give the zombie frightening strength – usually a little beyond that of a normal person – and their undead condition usually means that they cannot easily be destroyed. Even when part of a zombie has been obliterated, other parts can still sometimes function and can attack those who seek to destroy it. Cutting it into small pieces might not render it immobile and the various fragments might draw themselves back together again to form a complete body – gruesome! The only sure way to stop an attacking zombie, therefore, is to completely destroy the entire body. Setting it on fire and burning it to ashes is probably the only certain way to erase it.

RIGHT *A terrifying crowd of zombies. Some think they rise up because of epidemics or plagues in the area.*

In some tales, there is also an unhealthy connection between zombies and cannibalism. Although this element does not appear in all forms of folklore, there are tales from the Caribbean that seem to suggest it and so it has found its way into zombie fiction and movies. It is said that in order to sustain itself, the zombie must feed on living human flesh and that this makes it as dangerous as any vampire or werewolf. This is one basis of the idea that zombies might come together in groups in order to attack and eat the living. This notion has driven the plot line of a number of books and movies that have appeared over recent decades and plays on underlying fears (and a morbid fascination!) in our society about all forms of the living dead.

If you encounter a zombie, it is safe to assume that it *will* attack; the best way to save yourself is to run!

Types of Zombie

The walking dead can take many forms, from the lurching, shambling figures of the Caribbean, to the shrouded, wrapped mummies, and the skeletal marbh bheo that walk Irish roads. How many have you encountered?

VOODOO ZOMBIES

Often, when we think of zombies, we also think of Voodoo — the dark worship of strange gods that is allegedly practiced on some Caribbean islands, in the shadowy bayou country of Louisiana, and among the gloomy inlets of the South Carolina Low Country.

As well as raising corpses from the dead, its followers are rumored to practice cannibalism, human sacrifice, and all sorts of malicious witchcraft, including raising the dead. But how true is this increasingly popular image of the Voodoo zombie?

Just what *is* Voodoo? Although it is actually the official religion of Benin (formerly Dahomey) in West Africa, the word "Voodoo" is an umbrella term and covers a number of localized beliefs, many of which are West African, although some are from Cuba and South America. These beliefs include Mami Wata, Santeria, Arara, Mayombe, Palo, Lacumi, and even some forms of Christianity, and are often concerned with healing or fortune telling. But there is a dark side to them, too, and this is what has given Voodoo its sinister reputation.

Contained within certain of these beliefs is the power to curse or to do supernatural harm to someone. Voodoo priests, *bokors* or *houngans* (male) and *mambos* (female), are said to have the power to cast spells that may injure or even kill their enemies. They are also reputed to be skilled with herbs and poisons, and can make potions that give the appearance of death. These herbs can also take away a person's mind and make him or her act almost like a robot, obeying any command.

RIGHT *New Orleans Voodoo is thought to take place in the sinister swamps of the Louisiana bayou.*

Such powerful concoctions are sometimes known as "poudres" or Voodoo poisons. They are the basis for many zombie legends. People whose minds have been destroyed by these poisons are said to become the slaves of zombie masters and carry out their often extremely malicious instructions.

Because Voodoo relies on such a number of localized beliefs, there are a number of types. For example, there is a Haitian and Caribbean form found in Haiti and places such as Honduras and Barbados. Another type is to be found in Cuba and in certain South American countries, while yet another (known as New Orleans Voodoo)

LEFT *A Voodoo priest in Togo, West Africa. When other religions spread, many thought that Voodoo would not survive – but they were wrong!* RIGHT *A Voodoo shrine in a Togo local market.*

exists in Louisiana and areas of South Carolina. Much of Voodoo is associated with black slaves who were brought mainly from West Africa in the 1700s and 1800s to work in the Caribbean and North American plantations. However, there is also supposedly a white form of the belief known as "hoodoo" that is practiced in the stunning Ozark Mountains of Arkansas.

Caribbean Voodoo is divided into two forms – Rada and Petro. Rada is the oldest form of the belief and the name is taken from the area of Arada, a place in Benin in Africa, from which many of the original slaves were brought to work on French plantations in the Caribbean. This Voodoo is largely concerned with healing and prophesy, as well as communicating with the spirits and ghosts of people's long dead ancestors.

The Petro variation is associated more with the later Spanish plantations. The story is that a young slave, supposedly named Don Pedro, drank a lethal mixture of rum and gunpowder, then began an ecstatic dance. During this, the spirits possessed him. Ever since, the "Danse de Don Pedro" is a central feature of Petro ritual and gives rise to an uninhibited form of worship. It is also largely in the Petro beliefs that we find the idea of curses known as *gris-gris* (hideous charms) – some of which are made out of human remains – and the belief in zombies.

But the word "zombie" actually comes from the Rada tradition and does not refer to the walking dead at all. This tradition is much more developed than the wild and abandoned Petro, and has its own system of gods and goddesses. The greatest of these is thought to be Damballah Wedo (also known as Bondye from the French "*le bon dieu*" – the good god). He often appears as a great serpent (snakes tend to be venerated in Rada worship) that is known as "Le Gran Zombi." Damballah often

LEFT *A handmade Voodoo doll from New Orleans. It was used for the promotion of peace and tranquility.*

RIGHT *A model of the Voodoo serpent spirit, Damballah Wedo, father of all* loa.

communicates with his followers through beings named *loa* (spirits or ghosts), which may be dead ancestors or maybe even demons. These have the power to possess both people and objects in order to make the god's wishes known. This means that some *loa* have the power to raise corpses and to make them move as though alive. The *loa* can be commanded by *bokors* and *mambos*, who use them for whatever purpose they choose, including mobilizing the dead.

The traditions of Rada and Petro Voodoo often mingled on the plantations and the idea of the zombie crossed from one into the other. In both traditions there are believed to be individuals known as zombie masters – Voodoo priests with the specific power over the *loa* to make them raise the dead and carry out their wishes.

There are, according to some, a group of sorcerers somewhere in Haiti known as the "Cultes des Mortes" (the Cult of the Dead) who exist to do evil through the raising of the dead and the control of zombies. It was the "Cultes des Mortes" who were said to supply living dead men as part of the dreaded Ton Ton Macoute (the name means "Uncle Gunnysack," the name of a feared Haitian bogeyman), the secret police who operated in the country during the reign of the dictator François (Papa Doc) Duvalier (1957–1971). Many of them were said to be zombies. This is doubtful, but of course, many believed it to be true.

RELIGIOUS AND CULTURAL ZOMBIES

Where does the idea of the zombie come from and how did it start? Much of our zombie lore comes from the old slave religions of Africa and mostly from the west of the continent.

In the 16th, 17th, and 18th centuries, European and American ships raided the African coastline and carried off slaves to work in the French, Spanish, and English plantations of the Caribbean. The slaves brought with them some of the old, dark, pagan religions that had flourished in their homeland for centuries, and merged them with the largely Christian traditions of their masters.

Some of these beliefs were very strange and promoted the ideas of gods and spirits at work in the world, sometimes for good and sometimes for evil. For example, it was believed by some that people and even things might be possessed by these spirits. This sometimes included the bodies of the dead. The gods, the ghosts of ancestors, or the spirits of the forest might be called by a priest or magician and, with ritual and spells, might be encouraged to inhabit a body and make it appear to live. It was from this idea that the notion of the zombie was probably born – a dead cadaver brought to a kind of "life" by the dark powers, the origins of which lay deep in the African jungle.

Gradually, the slave religions began to take on elements of the European mainstream faiths, most notably French and Spanish Catholicism. While not completely ignored, the ghostly spirits of the forest were sometimes replaced by Catholic saints and by European specters that might also take over the bodies of the African dead and use them for whatever purposes the priests or magicians dictated.

ABOVE LEFT *Slaves, captured in West Africa, were shipped to the Americas in chains. Many died en route.*
RIGHT *Conditions onboard ship were horrific. But the slaves' Voodoo beliefs were strong and they took them with them.*

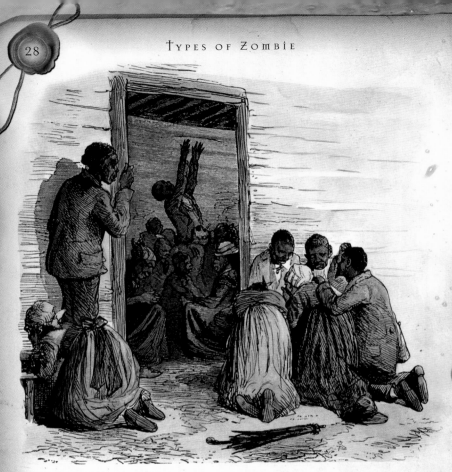

And of course, the Caribbean islands were not the only places in which these religions – and also the zombies – were to be found. America had its own slave population. Groups of them worked in the cottonfields of the southern states and in the rice plantations of South Carolina. Here, the slave beliefs mingled freely with the

ABOVE *A secret prayer meeting takes place on a plantation. Many plantation owners were terrified of the old religions. They worried that they would unsettle their workers, who would not then perform adequately on the estate.*

traditions of the plantation owners and gave rise to a belief that embraced both African traditions and Christian superstition. Ghosts and angels played a large part in such a belief system and were worshiped as part of it. The idea of rising from the dead – a central feature of Christian belief – also fed into the notion of the zombie. In America, the slave religion became known as "hoodoo" and was widely feared in such large slave cities as Charleston and New Orleans.

Most of the rituals that the slaves carried out on the various plantations – including the raising of zombies – were conducted in secret in hidden places in remote areas of the slave owners' property, or in the cane fields. No white eyes were supposed to see them. Of course, this led to the belief among the white slave owners that the worshipers were working against them. The frequent rumors of cannibalism and of the walking dead also terrified the white families who lived on the plantations. They instructed their overseers and the local authorities to clamp down on these pagan gatherings, but this only had the effect of making the worship more secretive.

There were widespread rumors of large groups of zombies who might attack the plantation house and kill (and perhaps eat) all who dwelt there – and this was a very real fear. Indeed, it is said that even today these undying armies are waiting in the swamps and bayous for their unsuspecting victims.

BELOW *An idyllic image of a plantation where all seems right with the world. But worries about slave uprisings, as well as zombies, often plagued the slave owners.*

THE MUMMY

The mummy shares many zombie characteristics – the shambling walk, the robotic manner, and the often murderous intentions.

Mummies are dead bodies – sometimes those of kings or very important people, sometimes those who have been ritually killed – that have been specially preserved. This is usually done by secret chemical processes known to the ancient peoples, or else by the conditions in the place where they have lain for many years.

THE MUMMY'S CURSE

☥ AS FOR ANYBODY WHO SHALL ENTER THIS TOMB IN HIS IMPURITY: I SHALL RING HIS NECK AS A BIRD'S.

☥ AS FOR ANY MAN WHO SHALL DESTROY THESE, IT IS THE GOD THOTH WHO SHALL DESTROY HIM.

☥ AS FOR HIM WHO SHALL DESTROY THIS INSCRIPTION: HE SHALL NOT REACH HIS HOME. HE SHALL NOT EMBRACE HIS CHILDREN. HE SHALL NOT SEE SUCCESS.

Mummies are are mainly to be found in Egypt, where the corpses of long dead rulers were laid to rest in great tombs ready for their mammoth journey to the afterlife.

Many such mummies date back thousands of years; the oldest known so far is thought to be from 3300 B.C. Because these mummies were so perfectly preserved, it was believed that, like the zombie, they could be brought back to a form of life by a series of spells or incantations that were known only to Egyptian sorcerers or possibly to their descendants.

Again, like the zombie, the mummy really had no will of its own and walked about blindly, until commanded by someone

Right A mummy who has risen from the dead is not someone you would want to meet on a dark night!

who had power over it. It is recorded that a grisly process, using sticky, black bitumen, a substance called natron (soda ash), and various herbs and perfumes, was carried out by specialized practitioners. In some cases, the dead body, especially if it was that of a king or queen, was then wrapped in linens to preserve it, and this has become the familiar image for us of the lurching mummy swathed in disintegrating bandages.

Even though mummies were generally guided by the magic priests who controlled them, some of them may possibly have been capable of some very simple form of independent, rational thought.

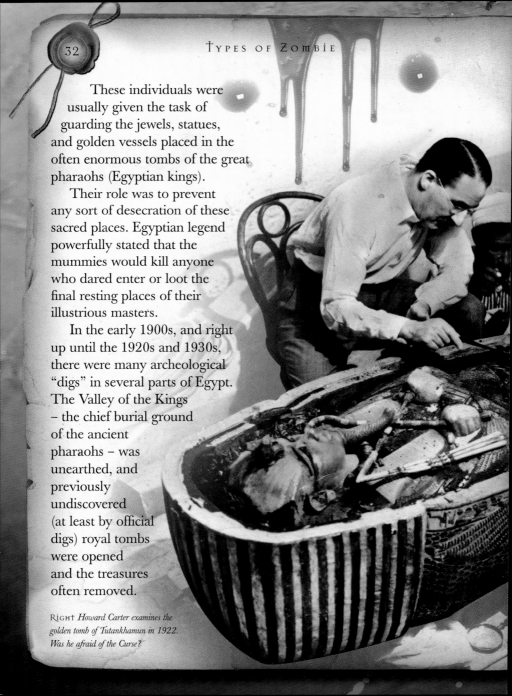

These individuals were usually given the task of guarding the jewels, statues, and golden vessels placed in the often enormous tombs of the great pharaohs (Egyptian kings).

Their role was to prevent any sort of desecration of these sacred places. Egyptian legend powerfully stated that the mummies would kill anyone who dared enter or loot the final resting places of their illustrious masters.

In the early 1900s, and right up until the 1920s and 1930s, there were many archeological "digs" in several parts of Egypt. The Valley of the Kings – the chief burial ground of the ancient pharaohs – was unearthed, and previously undiscovered (at least by official digs) royal tombs were opened and the treasures often removed.

Right *Howard Carter examines the golden tomb of Tutankhamun in 1922. Was he afraid of the Curse?*

During this period, stories of the gruesome and mysterious deaths of many who had entered these sites were widespread. The most famous discovery – and the most famous curse – occurred in 1922 with the excavation of the tomb of the boy pharaoh Tutankhamun by the archeologist Howard Carter.

Carter's patron was the British Lord Carnarvon, who entered the tomb with Carter. A year later, Carnarvon was dead – some said by the Curse of the Mummy. In fact, it is more likely that he died of blood poisoning, the result of an infected mosquito bite.

A number of other members of the team died in mysterious circumstances too. It was even claimed that some of them were strangled by a mummy – although this later proved to be unfounded.

But not even oceans can deter the mummies; further unexplained deaths have occurred in Europe and America, where ancient coffins have been transported.

Is there any place that is safe from these hulking creatures?

RIGHT *One of the most popular Egyptian cults was of the cat goddess Bast. Many cats were mummified for her.*

Although mummies are almost always associated with ancient Egypt, other cultures had them too. In fact, examples of the oldest mummies, the Chinchorro mummies from around 5050 B.C., have been found in the Andes Mountains in Chile and also in parts of Peru. Some of their internal organs have been removed, including the brain, and replaced with animal hair and plant fibers, giving them a kind of continuous "growing" life. These "living corpses" were not only those of great rulers, as was usually the case in ancient Egypt, but also of ordinary people – men, women, children, and, strangely, even miscarried fetuses. This suggests that the Andean peoples probably

BELOW *This man's body was found in 1900 in a bog on the borders of the Netherlands and Germany. He is called "Red Franz" because of his red hair.*

believed that everyone might return from death at some distant time.

Among the Incas of ancient South America, the bodies of those who were sacrificed to the gods were considered to be sacred and were therefore mummified. The Inca mummies are extremely old, and fall into two types, the Inca rulers and those who were sacrificed to the gods. Some experts have suggested that people thought that some of these sacrificial victims might at some time return from the realm of the gods and take over their bodies again.

The most famous mummy was nicknamed Juanita the "Ice Maiden" because, after she had been sacrificed, she was frozen beneath the high snows of Mount Ampato in Peru. She was discovered, perfectly preserved, in September 1995 when a nearby volcano erupted and thawed her out.

Although the process by which these Inca mummies were made is still not fully understood, it is thought that the dry mountain air played a vital part in creating them, making them "natural mummies" created by the environment.

The ancient peoples of the British Isles, and northern Europe too, believed in a process of "natural mummification" for their ritually slain bodies; these unfortunate people were usually strangled and dumped in a peat bog, where the natural elements would preserve them. The acids contained in the peat actually "pickled" the body, preserving it like a mummy.

These ritually sacrificed mummies are to be found all over northern Europe, the most famous being Tollund Man in Denmark and Lindow Man in England. They are so well preserved that they seem ready to walk from their graves into the living world. Other mummies have been found in China, Russia, and even the Canary Islands. Mummies, it seems, are to be found everywhere, lurking in our nightmares for years to come!

THE GOLEM

Zombies are usually regarded as a fundamental piece of Caribbean folklore, but several other traditions have similar eerie figures.

In Jewish lore, for example, we find references to the Golem, and this frightening figure is not very different from our idea of a zombie. It is a huge, shambling, humanlike clay figure that usually obeys the commands of the person who has created it and mostly lacks any intelligence of its own.

In the Jewish religion only God can create life, but some of the mystical words and symbols that God uses to do so have apparently been passed down to some very holy rabbis (religious teachers). Some of these are even said to have been written down in a text called the *Sefer Yitzirah* (Book of Formation) which has been hidden away but may still be accessible to certain rabbis.

Texts claiming to be part of the Book and its companion the *Zohar* (Book of Splendor) have been in circulation since medieval times. The formula was said to be that which God had first used to create Adam Kadmon (sometimes known as the primal man).

LEFT *Mystical words and symbols in the* Sefer Yitzirah.
RIGHT *An innocent child offers a Golem an apple. Let's hope the Golem does not run amok and kill everything in its path!*

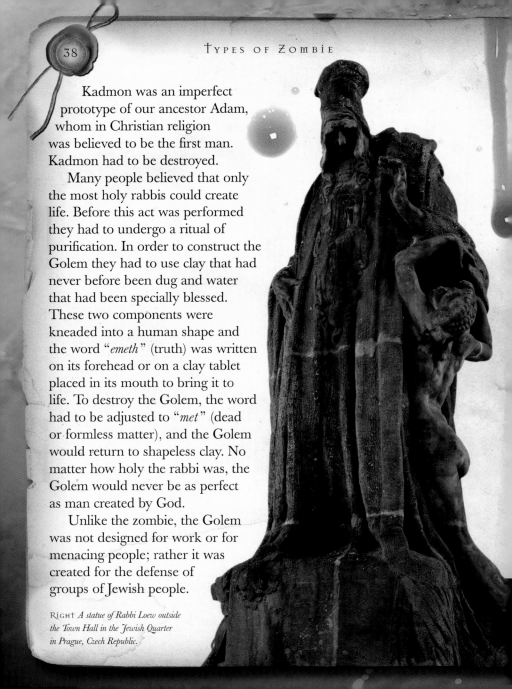

Kadmon was an imperfect prototype of our ancestor Adam, whom in Christian religion was believed to be the first man. Kadmon had to be destroyed.

Many people believed that only the most holy rabbis could create life. Before this act was performed they had to undergo a ritual of purification. In order to construct the Golem they had to use clay that had never before been dug and water that had been specially blessed. These two components were kneaded into a human shape and the word "*emeth*" (truth) was written on its forehead or on a clay tablet placed in its mouth to bring it to life. To destroy the Golem, the word had to be adjusted to "*met*" (dead or formless matter), and the Golem would return to shapeless clay. No matter how holy the rabbi was, the Golem would never be as perfect as man created by God.

Unlike the zombie, the Golem was not designed for work or for menacing people; rather it was created for the defense of groups of Jewish people.

RIGHT *A statue of Rabbi Loew outside the Town Hall in the Jewish Quarter in Prague, Czech Republic.*

The most famous story concerning the creature is believed to date from 16th century Europe and concerns the venerable rabbi Judah Loew ben Bezalel, the Chief Rabbi of Prague (also known as the Maharal of Prague). He is said to have created a Golem to protect the Jewish ghetto of the city from Christian attacks. According to the story, Rabbi Loew constructed the Golem out of clay taken from the banks of the Vlatva River and allowed it to roam the streets, defending the Jewish areas of the city. However, the creature became ever more violent, killing Gentiles as it went, and the Marharal began to lose control over it. The Emperor, Rudolph II, begged Rabbi Loew to destroy it, and the Maharal lured the Golem to the door of the strangely named Old New Synagogue in Prague, where he managed to extract the clay tablet from its mouth and change the word on it from "*emeth*" to "*met.*"

There are some who say that the Maharal did not actually destroy the creature but simply deactivated it, and that it still lies waiting for resurrection in the Synagogue's "*genizah*" (a place where old books are stored), where no one is allowed to go. This supposedly true tale was recorded in a diary by the rabbi's son-in-law. This record was said to have been lost but was allegedly found in Warsaw in 1909 by Yudi Rosenberg. It has become known as the *Katz Manuscript*. Some scholars think it's a fake. Maybe!

RIGHT *This Golem mosaic, found in a backstreet in Prague, is one of many Golem depictions in this ancient city, still today full of myths and legends.*

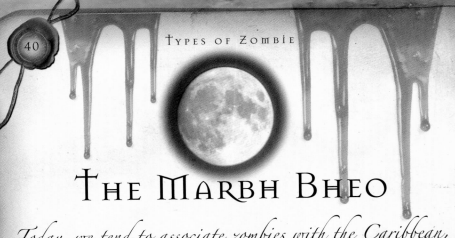

THE MARBH BHEO

Today, we tend to associate zombies with the Caribbean, Africa, and parts of South America, but perhaps one of the oldest forms of the walking dead comes from another part of the world — Ireland.

Here, the marbh bheo (the night-walking dead) often roamed the roads at certain times of the year, sometimes to take revenge for old grievances or sometimes just to return to the places they had known in life. Those who met them along lonely tracks and lanes might sometimes be taken back with them into the afterlife, so it was very wise to give them a wide berth.

Sometimes, however, these were the walking corpses of friends or relatives who had been allowed by God to return for a specific night of the year, such as Halloween or May Eve, to enjoy the things that they had in life. They could eat and drink, or enjoy music, which they could also play. The one thing that the marbh bheo could not do was to speak, in case they recounted to the living what the afterlife was like and what befell humans after death. Usually they had a bite to eat or a glass of whiskey, and enjoyed the activity of the house going on around them, for there was no great

RIGHT *The presence of the marbh bheo is felt all over Ireland, in folk tales and songs, as well as place names such as "Glan na Scail" (Valley of the Phantoms).*

fear connected with some of them. When the family slept, they often returned to their graves.

However, not all of them were kindly. Some of these corpses might return in order to do someone harm or to settle old scores. Nasty and vindictive people were often believed to become marbh bheo and to return in order to torment their families and neighbors. These were to be feared since they were only concerned with evildoing.

Unlike Caribbean zombies, there was no real dark magic involved in the rising from the grave of these creatures. Some believed God allowed them to rise through a special dispensation. These were known as the Blessed Dead and they had lived good lives. All others who rose were commanded by the Devil or by evil designs. So when the moon is full in Ireland, it is wise to stay indoors and keep well away from the roads at night.

ZOMBIE TALES

Do zombies really exist? Certainly there are a number of tales of Voodoo, slave rebellion, and of mysterious witchcraft in isolated places. Could there be zombies nearby? Decide for yourselves!

Zombie Masters

In the Caribbean, people do not believe that the zombie simply rises up from the grave and wanders about aimlessly. Rather, it is called from the tomb by a bokor (wizard or conjurer) or mambo (witch) who forces it to do their bidding.

At the heart of Caribbean zombie lore are strange and magical substances that are called Voodoo poisons. These are special concoctions that can be given to a living person either in his or her food or in a drink. They will rob the person of their senses and slow their bodily functions, making them appear to be dead. Many of these poisons are so strong that they have fooled doctors, who have pronounced the individuals deceased. However, they are not really dead, and when they have been buried with due ceremony, the magician returns and summons them from the grave. The person rises up as a zombie and is

RIGHT *Watch out for vengeful zombies like these, fooled into drinking Voodoo poisons and thus dying before their time.*

thereafter condemned to obey all the instructions of the conjurer.

In islands such as Haiti, it has been recounted that many of these "resurrected" zombies were sold to plantation owners to work on their property as unpaid servants. They were said to work tirelessly and obey every instruction given to them, and as long as they were fed the Voodoo poison regularly they were passive. They were never, however, to be fed salt, as this would counteract the effects of the poison and in their confused state the zombies might turn violent.

Even a small amount of salt was believed to have an effect.

Throughout the Caribbean, people with the power to raise zombies, whether it was as their own servants or to sell as slaves, were called zombie masters since they controlled all the walking dead.

According to some sources, there were groups of them on certain islands who forged a thriving trade out of the practice. And everyone was in danger, for they were continually on the lookout to find people to "zombify." So if you visit a Caribbean island, be on your guard and watch what you eat and drink!

OSIRIS AND HORUS

The idea of raising someone from the dead goes far back into the mists of time. Such stories may disguise a deeper meaning.

In ancient Greece, there are stories of people traveling into the Underworld to bring someone back from the dead – Orpheus raising his beloved wife Eurydice, for example. Such stories are certainly myths and fables. But were some ancient peoples actually able to raise the dead?

One of the first stories that we have comes from ancient Egypt. One of the oldest gods in their pantheon of deities, Osiris, was "resurrected" from the dead in physical form. The earliest reference to this event comes from a very old group of writings known as the *Pyramid Texts* and dates from around 2400 B.C. In the most widespread version of the story, Osiris was tricked by his evil brother, Set, who made him climb into a coffin that Set then sealed and threw into the Nile River. The coffin was found by Osiris's wife, Isis.

In some versions of the tale, Set tore up his brother's body and scattered it all over Egypt. Isis patiently searched until she had found every single piece and then reassembled her beloved husband.

Using a very ancient ritual, she was able to bring Osiris back to life, and she lived with him and bore him a son, Horus, who was worshiped as the God of the Sun. Because of the circumstances of his birth, Horus had some very special powers, one of which was being able to raise the dead. He is often portrayed – as is his other incarnation, Ra – as a powerful king with a crook and flail, and many pharaohs claimed him as their ancestor, and through him also Osiris. Could these descendants also raise the dead?

RIGHT *The god Osiris, in one piece again, sits enthroned in the Underworld, tended by Isis and her sister, Nephthys.*

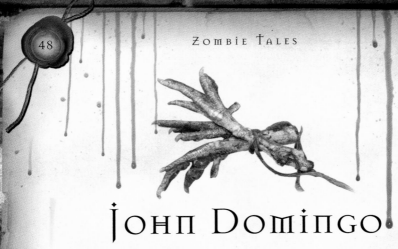

John Domingo

Of all the Voodoo magicians who lived in the U.S. city of Charleston in South Carolina, none was more powerful or more feared than John Domingo, "The Black Constable." In the late 1880s, his name was whispered everywhere in the city and even in the countryside beyond.

It was said that Domingo had originally been a slave on the rice plantations in the South Carolina Low Country, but that he had come to Charleston to live in a queerly shaped, shabby old house on Magazine Street, right at the corner of Mazyck Street (although it doesn't have that name today). It was a time when there were many Voodoo men, *ju-ju* doctors, and zombie masters in Charleston – people such as Cut-bread Jack who lived on Charlotte Street, or Dicky Breaux from the Dorchester Road, who both claimed they had great powers, including the raising of the dead. John Domingo, however, quickly became much more famous than either of them.

Domingo was a tall and well-built man who usually went about wrapped in a heavy Union Army greatcoat. His hair was long and dirty and hung around his face. On the fourth finger of his right hand he wore a large silver ring, carved in the shape of a snake, which he referred to as "Le Gran Zombie," claiming that it had been forged in the African Congo and that it had the power to raise the dead. Using this ring, it was said that Domingo carried out terrible Voodoo rituals in the old house on Mazyck Street – said to be built on the site of an old graveyard, although this is probably not the case. Here, he raised up bodies and sent them out through Charleston.

They had to perform various missions, usually to kill Domingo's enemies. A large number of people who spoke out against him died in suspicious circumstances – possibly at the hands of a zombie?

ABOVE LEFT *Chicken feet used in Voodoo spells have a variety of functions, anything from keeping someone silent to bringing good luck.*
BELOW *Charleston in 1900. Popular with zombie masters because of its past African slave inhabitants, whose descendants might also be believers.*

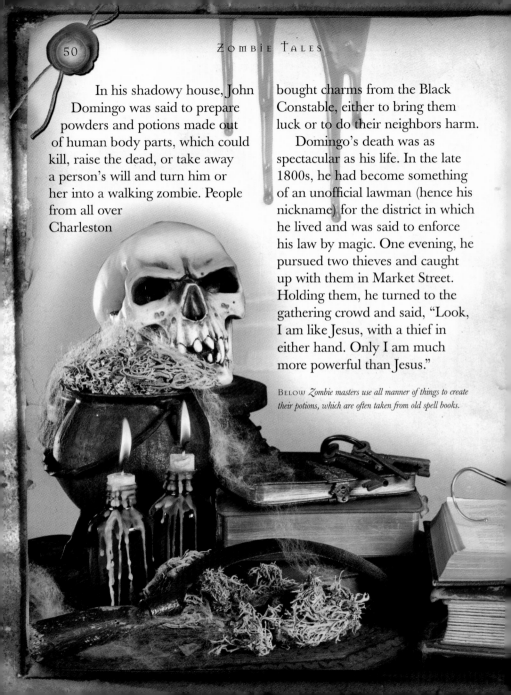

In his shadowy house, John Domingo was said to prepare powders and potions made out of human body parts, which could kill, raise the dead, or take away a person's will and turn him or her into a walking zombie. People from all over Charleston bought charms from the Black Constable, either to bring them luck or to do their neighbors harm.

Domingo's death was as spectacular as his life. In the late 1800s, he had become something of an unofficial lawman (hence his nickname) for the district in which he lived and was said to enforce his law by magic. One evening, he pursued two thieves and caught up with them in Market Street. Holding them, he turned to the gathering crowd and said, "Look, I am like Jesus, with a thief in either hand. Only I am much more powerful than Jesus."

BELOW *Zombie masters use all manner of things to create their potions, which are often taken from old spell books.*

He was going to say something else but suddenly he stopped. A look of bewilderment crossed his face and he seemed to rise up on his toes as if pulled upright by someone or something unseen. Some people claimed that they saw long and inhuman fingers on his windpipe. Falling to the ground, he appeared to age rapidly and die. He was carried to a local butcher's shop and seemed to shrink and wither. Later, his body was removed, and nobody knows where he is buried. His ghost is said to be seen striding along the streets of Charleston with his silver Congo ring – the ring that could allegedly raise the dead – flashing. The great zombie master may not be at rest!

DR. BUZZARD

The South Carolina Low Country has always boasted a good number of conjure men, ju-ju doctors, and zombie masters. One of the most famous of all of these was Stephaney Robinson, who was also known as "Dr. Buzzard" — the nickname had been passed down across the years from one conjure man to another.

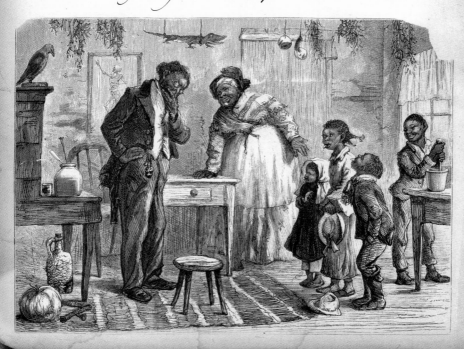

LEFT *The Oaks plantation where Dr. Buzzard is reputed to have lived in comfort – it was quite unusual at the time for an African-American to live in such style.*

Many stories are told about Dr. Buzzard – how he could cure or curse simply by looking at a person over the edge of the blue sunglasses that he usually wore. This was particularly useful when it came to his various court trials, as he could often confuse witnesses with this action. Another story was that he visited isolated churchyards out in the swamps in order to raise corpses there. In the early 1940s, he is described as an elderly, dapper little man in a black suit, who might well have been mistaken for a minister.

Ed McTeer, who succeeded his father as County Sheriff in 1926, came from a family of rice planters and was said to have witnessed the activities of the conjure men and zombie masters. His grandmother was said to have possessed the gift of prophesy. So the sheriff imagined himself the equal of Dr. Buzzard in magical terms.

The two of them embarked on a kind of war throughout the late 1930s and 1940s. Dr. Buzzard, without any doubt, appeared to win the majority of the skirmishes.

D r. Buzzard, who died early in 1947, lived in some comfort on the prestigious St. Helena Island in Beaufort County. He was known far and wide throughout South Carolina and beyond as a "root doctor" who made "poudres" (powders) and potions, some of which it was said could raise the dead. Part of his fame comes from a magical feud that he had with the High Sheriff of Beaufort County, J. E. McTeer, who, although having Celtic roots, fancied himself as a sorcerer and witch doctor.

LEFT Root doctors were still much sought after even in the 20th century – orthodox medicine was too expensive. Mostly they just treated simple ailments.

ABOVE *Python heads, eagle claws, or talons, and other such choice items are very popular and are believed to make effective Voodoo potions and remedies!*

For instance, McTeer tried to bring Dr. Buzzard to trial for giving young Gullah men (so called because their ancestors had been slaves from Angola) certain potions to help them escape being called up for army service in World War II. One of these men, Crispus Green, had actually died, supposedly from taking one of these potions, and McTeer tried to charge the doctor with murder. He failed as the real guilty party was found.

The turning point came, however, when Dr. Buzzard's son, a reckless character, drove his car off the road and was drowned in a creek. He was rumored to be drunk. Nevertheless, Dr. Buzzard believed that it was all down to McTeer's "hex" (curse) and strove to cut a deal with the sheriff.

It was struck but didn't last. Although he'd promised not to, Dr. Buzzard was soon practicing Voodoo again and said to be raising the dead in cemeteries. He continued to do so until his death in 1947.

Ed McTeer remained as High Sheriff of Beaufort County for

almost another twenty years. In 1960, however, he was challenged for the post by a South Carolina highway patrol sergeant, and his dubious reputation as a conjure man and zombie master counted against him. The idea was strengthened when a television broadcast made by his opponent was mysteriously interrupted by unknown interference. The patrolman won but did not enjoy a long career, eventually

going wild, barricading himself in his house, and threatening suicide. He was finally placed in a mental institution for his own safety. Had McTeer driven him mad?

The story of the feud has passed into Low Country folklore. Are there still zombies in the swamps created by the man in the black suit?

BELOW *The beautiful but eerie South Carolina swamplands are today a sanctuary for animal and plant life. Are they also ideal hangouts for zombies?*

MARIE LAVEAU

Perhaps the most famous "Voodoo Queen" and zombie mistress in all of New Orleans was the celebrated Marie Laveau.

She styled herself "La Gran Mambo" and is supposed to have "reigned" in the city between the years 1794 and 1881, making her nearly 100 years old. Some say she was still living in 1918. Indeed, some people claim that she may have been over 150 years of age when she died, kept alive by her supernatural powers!

The actual truth may be that there were *three* Marie Laveaus, the first two of whom were mother and daughter. The third (whose real name was Malvina Latour) simply took the name for herself.

The original Marie ran what was known as a "Voodoo salon" on St. Ann Street, which ran between North Rampart Street and Burgundy Street, close to Congo Square in New Orleans. There were great gatherings of worshipers, attended by many white people and at which strange rituals were carried out. Marie presided over these like a queen, working spells and giving out charms to those who were prepared to pay for them and who had come to consult her. It was said that some of the "servants" who attended the revellers were zombies that she had raised in the St. Louis Cemetery and whom she controlled.

In the early to mid-1800s, a number of Voodoo workers lived in New Orleans and were often consulted by both black and white people. These included "magicians" such as Mama Eunice, Mama Calliba, Dr. Maurice, and Dr. Yah-Yah. They all claimed to be able to raise the dead by using such things as "goofer dust" (soil from a grave, mixed with special ingredients).

RIGHT *Marie Laveau was a handsome woman. She was not a slave but was of mixed blood. It was rumored she may have been the daughter of a French aristocrat.*

Some of these people lived at the same time as Marie and were her enemies, seeking to overthrow her and take away her clients. Marie, however, outmaneuvered them all. It is said that this was because she had been taught by one of the greatest New Orleans sorcerers of them all – Dr. John (or "Old John Bayou" as he was sometimes known), who had learned his magic in the deep, dark bayou country to the south of the city. The spirit of the great Voodoo man was said to reside in a huge snake that Marie always carried about with her at the gathering, and which she called "Le Gran Zombi." This snake gave greater influence to her spells and to the charms that she sold.

Stories about her were plentiful and she encouraged them all. As well as raising zombies from the cemetery, it was said that she could make a powerful love potion, sought after by many people, from the fragments of dead bodies and that she could cause sickness simply by wishing a person ill. From time to time, the local police raided Marie's establishment, but on every occasion she passed herself off as a hairdresser, and claimed that those who sought her Voodoo services were her clients.

Marie had a number of husbands but it's not clear who they all were. Two names are known. The first was Jacques Paris, whom she married in 1819 and who seems to have "vanished" about six years

LEFT *The "Wishing Stump" rumored to have been used by Marie Laveau. Money is left in the basket now but once it may have been "wishes."*

ABOVE *The small house on St. Ann Street where Marie lived and practiced her craft. It is now a Voodoo shop.*

after the marriage. Whether the circumstances were suspicious is not known. The second was Christophe Glapion, who moved in with her after Jacques' disappearance, and with whom she had at least one daughter – she later became Marie Laveau II. The three of them lived in the little house on St. Ann Street until Christophe's death in 1835, even though Marie was thought to have owned many grander properties, most of which were scattered all over New Orleans.

When she became too old to continue her work, her daughter took over the Voodoo practice until Marie's supposed death in 1881. Then Marie II was deposed by one Malvina Latour, who claimed to be another daughter and who became Marie III. However, by this time the interest in Voodoo was dying in New Orleans and Latour did not prosper. Nevertheless, the name and legacy of the original Marie Laveau is still whispered in the more shadowy corners of the city.

THE ZOMBIE MASTERS OF WALNUT HILLS

Along the road that runs between Cincinnati and Walnut Hills in Ohio, there stood in the late 1840s and early 1850s, a small shack which always looked as if it was ready to fall down.

Nobody knew who actually lived there, but it was said that very strange figures were frequently seen coming and going from the place, particularly around twilight and during the hours of darkness.

From time to time, too, a piece of cardboard would be placed on the door which carried the misspelled words "Chemical Labaratary." Local people tended to give the place a wide berth, saying that it was "haunted." Some people even claimed to have seen walking dead people in that particular area. It was believed that whoever dwelt there dealt with grave robbers who supplied dead bodies for experimentation. It was also claimed that a well-known local individual named "Old Cunny," who dealt in bodies, was seen around the cabin on certain nights of the year.

At last these sinister rumors reached the ears of the local law enforcement authorities, and when a number of people went missing around Walnut Hills, the police finally raided the hut late in 1852. Somebody must have tipped off whoever was there, for the place had been quickly abandoned. The police refused to release any details of what was found there, except to say that certain "dark robes" and "curious books" had been taken

RIGHT *In a dilapidated shack such as this, the zombie masters of Walnut Hills plied their terrifying trade. Maybe they still do somewhere in the region today!*

from the place. It was also said that human body parts (and even whole bodies) were discovered there. In the eyes of Puritan Ohio, this counted as "devil's work." It was whispered that the tumbledown shack had been used for the creation of zombies.

So who were the zombie masters? Many have speculated who they might have been, but even today nobody knows for sure.

CLAIRVIUS NARCISSE

In many Caribbean islands, zombies belong to the realms of mythology and folklore, but once in a while a real one shows up, just to reinforce the old stories and maybe frighten those who meet them. One of these encounters took place about thirty years ago on the island of Haiti.

In 1980, a Haitian man named Clairvius Narcisse, who had been dead and buried for eighteen years, suddenly wandered into a village on the far side of the island from the place where he'd been born. He seemed dazed and unfamiliar with the place, but spoke to those he met in a slow, halting way, asking where he was.

By coincidence, his sister Angela was living in this village and she recognized her "dead" brother right away. In his vague and very bewildered state, however, he did not recognize her.

He had been wandering around Haiti, he told the local authorities, for some time (some accounts say that it was as long as sixteen years) and had been working for various employers. Through all that time, he had been in a confused state and was not able to tell the authorities much about where he'd worked or the names of his employers.

He said that he'd been given a "poudre" (a medicine or drug) in 1962 by one of his brothers who was widely regarded as a powerful Voodoo *bokor* (witch doctor), after the two had an argument over some land. He remembered nothing more, but his sister Angela was able to tell the authorities that she recalled he'd collapsed with a "mysterious illness."

TOP LEFT *Clairvius Narcisse in old age. He was never able to give a full account of what had happened to him.* RIGHT *Another famous zombie of Haiti was Felicia Felix Mentor, who apparently died and was buried in 1907. She was found wandering in the countryside in 1937. This picture of her is thought to be the only photograph of a zombie.*

Two days later, Clairvius had been pronounced dead by two qualified doctors. He was then buried but perhaps later "resurrected" as a zombie by his

ABOVE *Wade Davis has investigated whether trances are caused by drugs.*
RIGHT *A macabre, but not unusual, Haitian gravestone.*

brother and sold to another *bokor* as a servant. He passed through a number of employers until the effects of the drug started to wear off and he was able to escape. He had wandered for days, unsure of where he was, until he had come to the village and been seen by his sister.

At first there was some suspicion about him – that he was an impostor and that the whole thing was a hoax – but he was identified by both Angela and another sister, Marie-Clare, and it is said that his death certificate was even produced.

Clairvius never fully recovered his senses. Until he died he

would remain in a confused state, sometimes wandering off. He was examined by many qualified local doctors who suggested that he might have been poisoned using some sort of unknown drug. The doctors thought it might have been given to him by his brother, and later in his food by the other *bokors* who had kept him as a slave. When the last of his masters died, he had received no more of the "magical potion" and had escaped. There seemed little doubt that he'd been given a very powerful Voodoo "poudre."

Clairvius' story fascinated several doctors, scientists, and anthropologists, who wanted to find out if such a "poudre" existed, and if so, what it was. The most famous of these was a Canadian anthropologist called Wade Davis, who wrote a best-selling book on his search for the "poudre" called *The Serpent and the Rainbow*. This was made into a film in 1988 by the director Wes Craven. Davis did not, however, find the drug and it has eluded others since. It was thought that the drug might have something to do with the calabar bean or even puffer fish organs, but these theories were quite inaccurate. Whatever the "resurrection powder" that Clairvius took might be, it remains a mystery to this day.

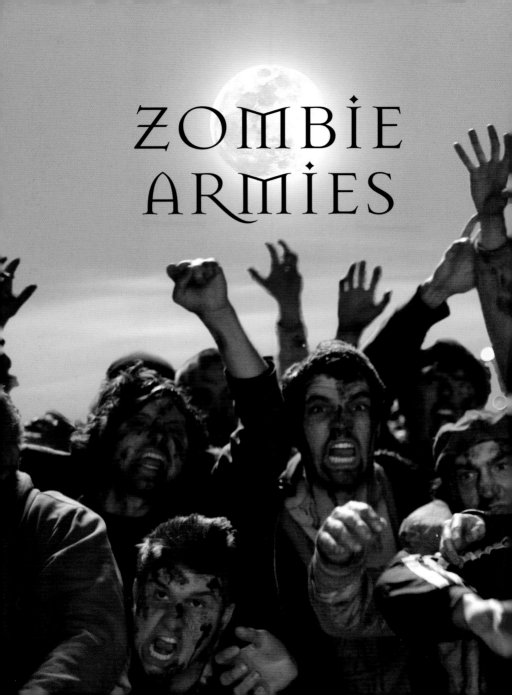

Although many believe that zombies follow the instructions of a zombie master, there are some people who believe that zombies can band together for various purposes, such as to attack the living. These are the rumored zombie armies that may be lurking in the shadows.

THE CAULDRON OF REBIRTH

Rising from the dead has often played an important part in Celtic folklore.

I ndeed, it was even believed by the Celts that there existed in ancient times a magical cauldron. If a body was placed in it, it would rise again as a living person. The vessel was called the Cauldron

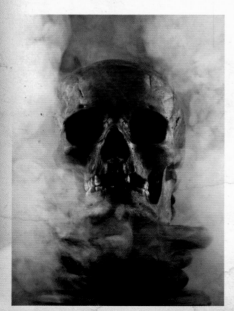

of Goibniu after a famous smith who had forged it from the helmet of a fallen god.

In the second branch of the *Mabinogion* (stories from medieval Welsh manuscripts) there is a story about the Cauldron, in which Branwen, the sister of Bran, an ancient British giant king, was given in marriage to Matholwch, an Irish ruler who took her back across the sea to live with him.

As part of her dowry, Matholwch demanded an ancient Cauldron that Bran held, which was said to be the Cauldron of Rebirth. It produced food and healed people, as well as restoring the dead to life, or so it was said. Bran gave it to him.

According to legend, Matholwch treated Branwen very badly, and news of her hardship reached the

LEFT *The dead need to be fresher than this to benefit from the Cauldron's life-giving powers!*

ABOVE *The Cauldron of Rebirth was in use after every battle to replenish the number of troops.*

ears of her half-brother Efnesin, who had been opposed to the marriage. Apart from Branwen's treatment, Matholwch wanted an excuse to lead an Irish army into Britain to dethrone Bran. After some British soldiers slew Irish nobles who were trying to sneak into the country and start a rebellion, a war broke out. The Cauldron given to Matholwch now became very important.

After each battle, the Irish simply gathered up their dead and threw them into the pot, and they sprang out alive again to fight the following day. However, Efnesin came up with a plan to counter this. He pretended to be dead, and was gathered up and thrown into the Cauldron, whereupon he extended his body and burst the vessel asunder. However, he died in the process.

Once the Irish were defeated, the cauldron fragments were buried. But if they were found, who knows what might happen?

Denmark Vesey and Gullah Jack

Through the plotlines of books and movies, we are now used to seeing armies of zombies attacking the authorities and slaughtering innocent people. But could that really happen? Back in 1822, one man thought it could. His name was Denmark Vesey.

In many respects, Vesey was a remarkable man. He was a slave of uncertain origin who had been bought in 1781 by Captain Joseph Vesey on the then-Danish-held Caribbean island of St. Thomas. The Captain kept him as a personal servant, gave him his own name, and taught him to read and write. However, he later sold him. Having briefly been a slave in the French colony of Saint Domingue (present-day Haiti), Vesey was taken to the U.S. port of Charleston where he would live until his death in 1822.

In 1799, Vesey had the most surprising stroke of luck. He won $1,500 (a large amount in those days) in a local lottery and was able to buy his freedom. With the rest of the money he started a branch of the African Methodist Episcopal Church in the city, which had a largely black congregation. The early 1800s were a time of slave uprisings on many plantations (the most serious being Nat Turner's Rebellion in Southampton County, Virginia, in 1831) and the white authorities became increasingly worried about Vesey's church. In 1820, they closed it down without warning, an action that angered him greatly.

Right *A rioter is hung alive by the ribs. The measures taken against the slaves were vicious, and the Vesey uprising did not help the slave cause.*

Vesey had been inspired by the 1791 Haitian Revolution, and he schemed to lead a slave revolt that would take over the entire port of Charleston and drive out the white people. He began to recruit an army from the plantations of South Carolina, but this recruitment was slow. Vesey was a free black man and many of the slaves didn't trust him – for instance, it was doubtful that he had been born in Africa, the birthplace of many slaves.

One of those he did recruit, however, was a slave owned by a local planter named Paul Pritchard. This slave was Gullah Jack (sometimes known as Couter Jack or Gullah Jack Pritchard), who came from Angola in Africa and was a great *bokor* or conjurer. Although supposedly a Methodist, it was said that Gullah Jack still practiced the old ways and that he was a zombie master and could raise the dead. He is supposed to have told Vesey that he could add to his army by creating a battalion of zombies. With Gullah Jack's influence, more and more Charleston slaves began to

join Vesey's movement and the plans for a rising began to take shape. In the meantime, it is said, Gullah Jack went about raising dead people to take part in the rebellion.

The uprising was set for Bastille Day, July 14, 1822. The plan was that the rebels and the zombies would rise up and kill their owners and many other white people, and take control of Charleston. Neither Vesey nor Gullah Jack intended to remain there afterward, but would travel to Haiti to join the new administration there. This did not sit well with some of the slaves, who still didn't trust Vesey, and two of them leaked the details of the plot to the authorities.

Over 131 men were arrested and brought to trial; of these, 67 were convicted, and 37 hanged. Denmark Vesey and Gullah Jack were hanged on June 23, bringing the slave revolt to an end and tightening white security in Charleston.

But what happened to the zombie army that Gullah Jack is supposed to have created? Perhaps it is still there, out in the misty South Carolina swamplands, waiting to be called into action, ready to attack and destroy.

LEFT *The 1791 slave revolt in Haiti was an inspiration to Denmark Vesey and Gullah Jack. Unlike their uprising, the Haiti revolt marked the start of the end of French rule.*

WILLIAM SEABROOK

Perhaps no person has added more to the lore of the zombie than William Seabrook (1884–1945). He certainly added to the fame of the island of Haiti as a center of zombie activity by bringing it to the attention of the world.

Born in Westminster, Maryland, William Seabrook started out as a journalist and newspaper editor in Georgia. He later became a travel writer and contributed to such well-known magazines as *Reader's Digest* and *Vanity Fair*. But it was while he was working on an assignment in West Africa among a tribe called the Guerre (whom he claimed were cannibals) that Seabrook became interested in Voodoo and secret African religions. He began to travel all over Africa, mainly in search of unusual and forbidden things, such as the Devil-worshiping Yezidi cults of the Arabian peninsula. He also drank very heavily and took a vast quantity and variety of drugs.

Hearing of zombies in the Caribbean, Seabrook went to the island of Haiti where he claimed to have made contact with the "Cultes des Mortes" (the group of zombie masters). He wrote a book, *The Magic Island*, about the place, and it became a best-seller. A particular section, "Dead Man Working in the Canefields," was frequently published in magazines in the U.S.A. The section was actually based on Article 246 of the Haitian Penal Code, which forbade the employment of walking corpses by local plantation owners.

Maybe because of what he'd discovered, Seabrook's mind began to collapse and he became an alcoholic. He struggled with this by admitting himself to several mental institutions. He married in 1935 but divorced only six years later. In 1945, he committed suicide by overdosing on drugs while living in Rhinebeck, New York. What did he know that perhaps we don't?

BELOW *Voodoo followers prepare the spot for a Voodoo ceremony in Port-au-Prince, Haiti. Haitians honor the Gede, spirits responsible for the dead.*

KNOW YOUR ENEMY

So now you think you will know a zombie when you meet one. But do you know what to do when that shape comes shambling toward you?

Y ou know that zombies were once everyday, ordinary people – your neighbors, your schoolmates, your family… But you must set your sympathies and loyalties aside.

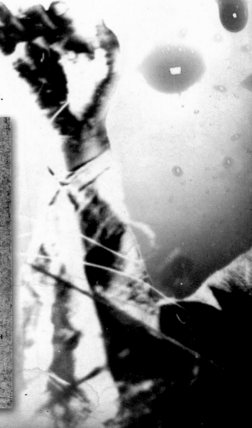

REMIND YOURSELF THAT ZOMBIES ARE:

◉ THE REANIMATED CORPSES OF SOMETIMES LONG-DEAD HUMANS.
◉ MINDLESS BEINGS WITHOUT REASON OR COMPASSION.
◉ INFECTED – BUT WITH WHAT WE STILL DO NOT KNOW.
◉ DEAD!

THIS MEANS THAT:
◉ THEY RESEMBLE THE PEOPLE YOU KNEW AND LOVED.
◉ YOU CANNOT REASON OR PLEAD WITH THEM IN ANY CIRCUMSTANCES.
◉ THEY CAN INFECT YOU.
◉ THEY ARE NOT AS SMART, FAST, OR CAPABLE AS YOU.

Most zombies are infected by other zombies, so do not head out into populated areas. Travel in small groups, as you will have a much higher chance of looking out for one another.

BELOW *No fear that you would mistake this for your best friend!*

Zombies will survive the loss of limbs, flesh damage, internal organ trauma – anything other than the destruction of the brain. The urge to feed often overrides all else, so the only way to deal with a zombie is to kill it before it kills you.

Now, there's a zombie at the door. If he gets in, you, and everyone with you, will die. Whoever the zombie once was is gone. Your only hope is to run or kill, and do it fast.

GLOSSARY

Bokor
A magician, often in Haitian Voodoo, who serves a *loa*. *Bokors* can practice both good and black magic.

Emeth
A word in Hebrew (the ancient language of Jews) that means "truth." It is used to activate a golem.

Grave robbers
People who rob graves or tombs in order to steal precious things buried with the body.

Gris-gris
A good luck charm. This is usually a small cloth bag, filled with herbs, oils, stones, bones, and so on, worn on the person to protect the wearer from harm.

Gullah
These were mostly slaves brought from Sierra Leone in West Africa, who settled in the Low Country of South Carolina. They have preserved much of their language and heritage.

Hex
Anything, such as a spell or curse, that brings bad luck.

Hoodoo
Hoodoo is a group of magical practices, usually practiced by African-Americans descended from slaves. It is sometimes known as "conjure."

Houngan
The male high priests in the Voodoo religion who serve the *loa*.

Ju-ju
Like the *gris-gris*, this is a protective charm. *Ju-ju* is an African word coming from the French word "joujou" (toy).

Loa
The spirits of the Voodoo religion. They are sometimes the spirits of ancestors. They are not prayed to, but served.

Magician
Like *bokors, mambos,* and *conjure* men, magicians have supernatural powers and can use these, and potions, to summon up zombies.

Mambo
The high priestess of the Voodoo religion. It is her responsibility to preserve the rituals and songs and keep up the relationship between the spirits and the community.

Met
A Hebrew word meaning "dead." It is used to deactivate a golem.

Mojo
Like the *gris-gris*, another hoodoo good luck charm. The bag is made of red cloth.

Mummification
This is a means of preserving the skin and organs of a body, either accidentally or intentionally, by chemicals, extreme cold, or lack of air.

Poudres
The French word for "powders," it refers to the potions created by the magicians and root doctors.

Root doctors
Hoodoo magicians. They make medicines, cast spells, give advice, create charms to deter evil and bring good luck.

Sorcery
It is the use of magical or supernatural powers.

Zuvembe
An African name for the "undead," a creature much like a zombie in Haitian Voodoo, who serves a *loa*.

İΠDEX

INDEX CONTINUED

ACKNOWLEDGMENTS

Marshall Editions would like to thank the following for their kind permission to reproduce their images:

t = top **b** = bottom **c** = center **r** = right **l** = left

Cover Credits: Front cover design by Ivo Marloh & Tim Scrivens – Jacket photos: Shutterstock/Getty Images

Pages: 1 Shutterstock/Dmitrijs Bindemanis; **3** Kobal Collection/Palace/Film4/BR Screen; **4-5** Shutterstock/Algol; **6** Alamy/ Darby Sawchuk; **7** Alamy/Photos12; **8** Photos12/Archives du 7eme Art; **9** Chad Savage; **10** Topfoto/The Granger Collection; **11** Corbis/Rykoff Collection; **12-13** Alamy/Archives du 7eme Art; **14b** Shutterstock/Tristan Tan; **14 -15** Shutterstock/Ljupco Smokovski; **16-17** Kobal Collection/Strike Entertainment/New Amsterdam/Michael Gibson; **18l** Shutterstock Damian Palus/Joe Belanger/Niderlander/Aleks.k; **18-19c** Kobal Collection/Lion's Gate Films/Creep Entertainment; **21** Shutterstock/Paul S. Wolf; **22** Alamy/Robert Estall Photo Agency/Carol Beckwith & Angela Fisher; **23** Art Directors/Trip/Jane Sweeney; **24** Topfoto; **25** Alamy/Louise Batalla Duran; **26** Corbis/ Bojan Brecelj; **27** Corbis; **28** Topfoto/The Granger Collection; **29** Corbis; **30** Corbis/ Poodles Rock; **32-33** Getty Images/Hulton Archive; **33r** Art Archive / Musèe du Louvre Paris/Dagli Orti; **34-35** Science Photo Library/Niedersachsisches Landesmuseum/Munoz-Yague; **36** Art Archive/University Library Istanbul/Dagli Orti; **37** Alamy/ AF Archive; **38** Alamy/William Manning; **39** Shutterstock/Peter Zurek; **40** Alamy/Nagelestock.com; **41** Andy Pacoriek; **42-43** Corbis/James Pomerantz; **44-45** Kobal Collection/Warner Bros/Peter Iovino; **47** Alamy/Ivy Close Images; **48** Shutterstock/ Knud Nielsen; **49** Getty Images/Buyenlarge; **50-51** Fotolia/Anyka; **52** Topfoto/The Granger Collection; **53** South Carolina Department of Archives & History; **54t** Alamy/Peter Arnold Inc; **54-55** Shutterstock/David Huntley; **57** Louisiana State Museum, Baton Rouge; **58** Voodoo Museum, New Orleans; **59** Vince Feliu/Sabreur76@Flickr; **61** Bridgeman Art Library; **62** public domain; **63** Alamy/Mary Evans Picture Library; **64** Corbis/ Joanna Vestey; **64-65** Photolibrary/Mauritius/Obert Obert; **66tl** Shutterstock; **66-67** Kobal Collection/Pariah Films; **68** Shutterstock/Dmitrijs Bindemanis; **69** Shutterstock/James Steidl; **71** Bridgeman Art Library/Archives Charmet; **72** Topfoto/The Granger Collection; **74** Corbis/Hulton-Deutsch Collection; **75** Reuters/Eduardo Munoz; **76-77** Mary Evans Picture Library/Ronald Grant Archive